READ TOGETHER

All About Giraffes

EDventure
LEARNING

How to Use This Book

This book is part of our Read Together series, a collection of books designed to be enjoyed by a young reader paired with a more experienced reader, such as a parent, grandparent, or older sibling. Take turns reading out loud together.

The pages on the left side are meant for the younger reader. These pages use short, simple sentences and larger print. They are marked at the bottom of the page with the symbol shown at left.

The right-side pages are for the older reader. They contain paragraphs with longer sentences and more complex vocabulary. These pages are marked at the bottom of the page with the symbol shown at right.

Shared reading helps new readers gain confidence. It's also a great way for all ages to bond over books. We hope you enjoy this book as you Read Together.

Printed in the United States of America
Paperback ISBN: 978-1-64824-011-9

EDventure Learning LLC
5601 State Route 31 #1296
Clay, NY 13039

www.edventurelearning.com
Email us at hello@edventurelearning.com

Table of Contents

What Giraffes Look Like

Giraffes are very tall.

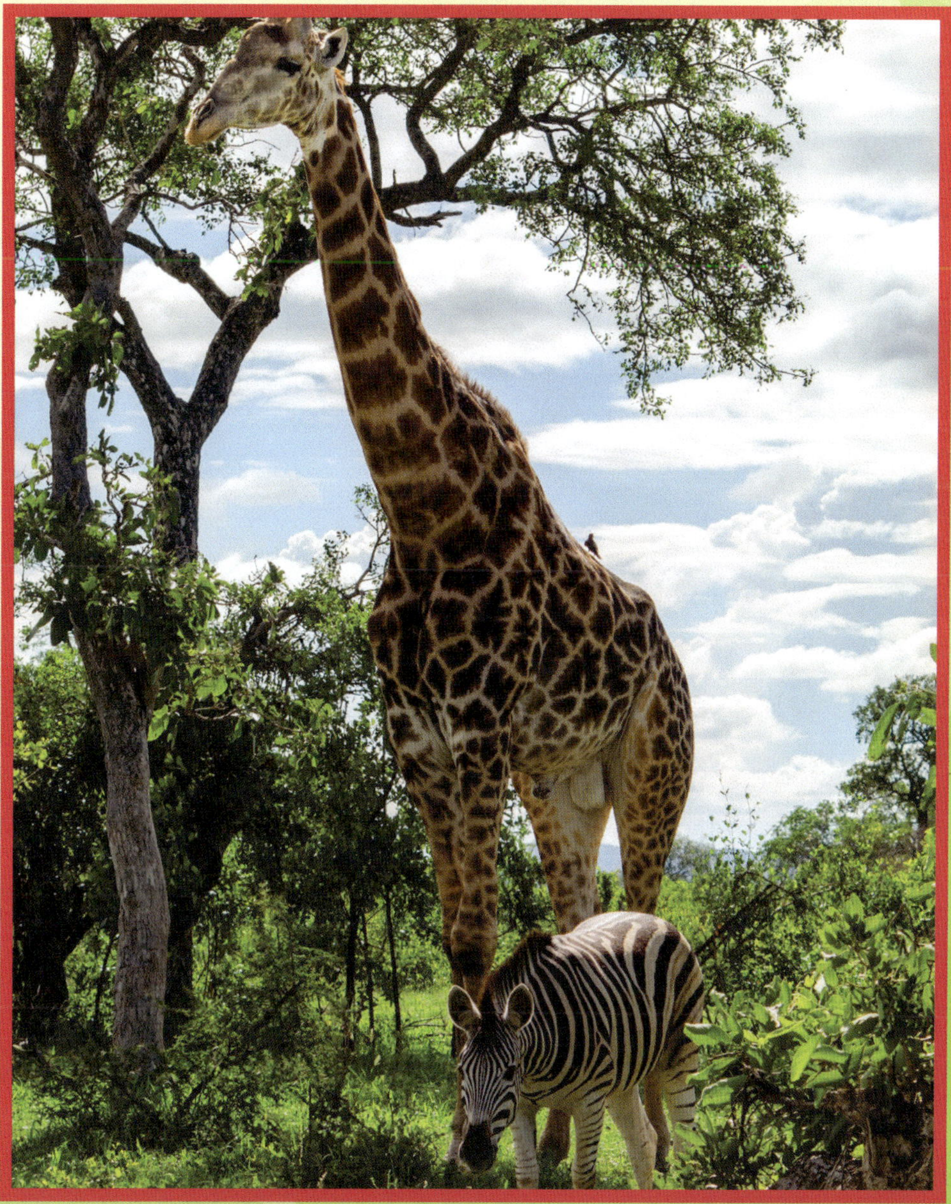

They are the tallest animals in the world. Adult giraffes are 14-19 feet (4-6 meters) tall. Being so tall lets them eat leaves that are high in the treetops. It also helps them spot predators from far off so they can run away.

Even baby giraffes are taller than most people.

A baby giraffe is called a **calf**. When a calf is born, it is already 6 feet (1.8 meters) tall and weighs over 100 pounds (45 kg). Giraffes are fully grown by the time they are 4-6 years old.

Long legs help giraffes run fast.

Giraffes have four long legs with hoofed feet. Most of the time, giraffes walk, but if they are trying to get away from a predator, they can move fast. Giraffes can run up to 35 miles (56.3 km) per hour!

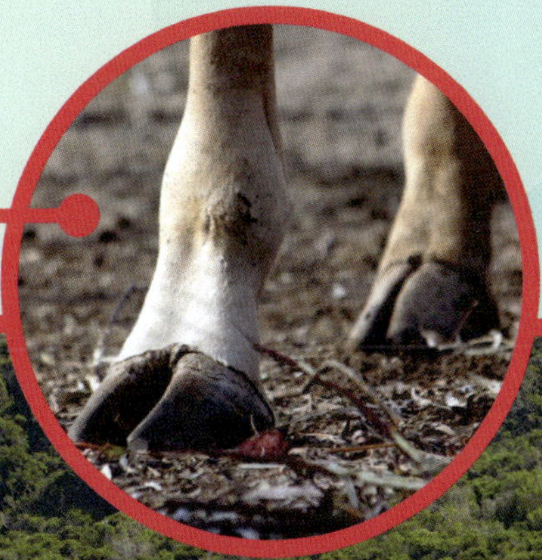

Giraffes have spots.

Giraffes are covered in coats of short fur with brown spots. Giraffes from the same area have similar spots, but no two giraffes have the exact same pattern. Each giraffe's spot pattern is one-of-a-kind, just like human fingerprints!

Giraffes have fuzzy bumps on their heads.

Those horn-like bumps on a giraffe's head are called **ossicones**, which means "bony cones." Unlike the horns or antlers of other animals, ossicones are covered with skin and fur, just like the rest of the giraffe's body.

Where Giraffes Live

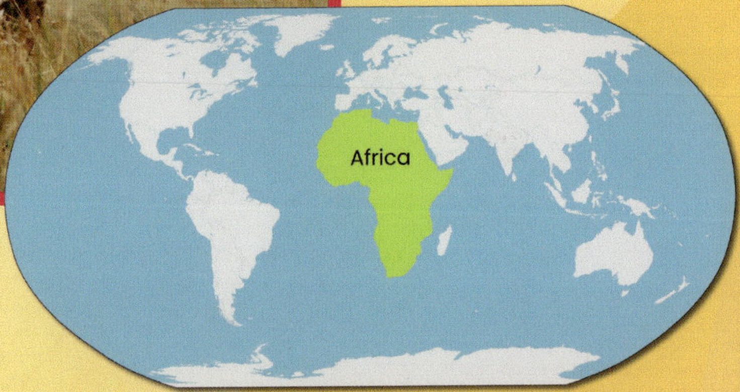

Giraffes live in Africa.

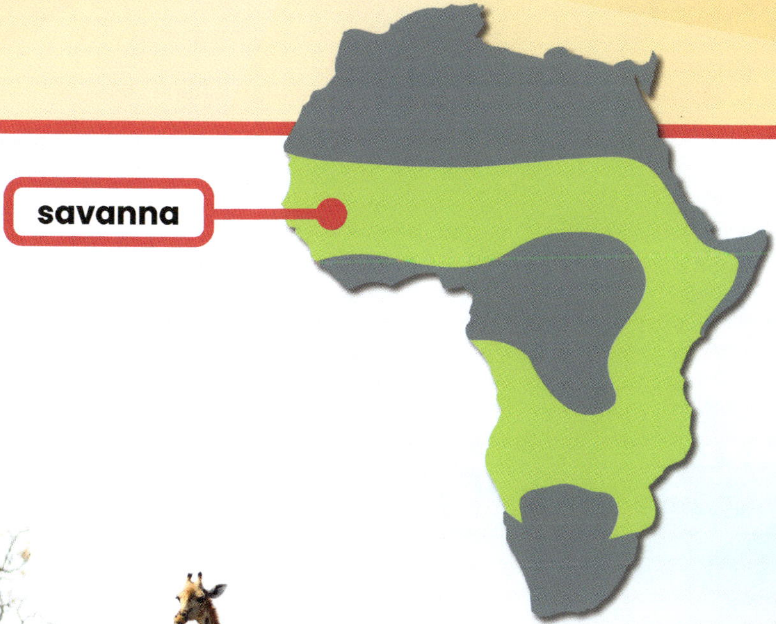

The type of land that giraffes live on is called the **savanna**. This land is made up of flat plains covered in tall grass and scattered trees. Many other animals live in the savanna, too, like zebras, elephants, and lions.

They live where it is warm.

The savanna is warm all year long, with temperatures from 64-86°F (17-30°C). From December to April is the dry season. The savanna gets hardly any rain.

From May to November is the wet season, when it rains a lot. This rain is needed to grow the plants that giraffes eat.

Giraffes need open space.

The wide-open savanna gives giraffes plenty of room to get around. It would be hard for them to move their huge bodies around in a thick forest. The spread-out trees in the savanna are just right for giraffes. They give giraffes enough food while still giving them lots of room. Flat, open land also makes it easier for giraffes to run if they need to escape predators.

What Giraffes Do

Giraffes eat plants.

Giraffes eat many kinds of plants, but their favorite foods are leaves from acacia trees. They reach up with their long necks and grab leaves with their huge tongues. It takes a lot of leaves to fill up such a big animal, so a giraffe spends almost its whole day eating.

They take short naps.

Giraffes eat so much that they don't even stop at night to sleep. In fact, the only time they sleep is in few tiny naps throughout the day that last around 5 minutes each. Usually, giraffes sleep standing up.

Giraffes do not drink very much water.

Drinking can be tough for giraffes. Their necks can't reach the ground when they are standing upright, so it's hard for them to get water. In order to reach the water, giraffes will either spread their front legs far apart or kneel down.

Luckily, giraffes don't have to get into this tricky position too often. They only need to drink once every few days. They get the rest of the water their bodies need from the leaves they eat.

Giraffes live in groups.

A group of giraffes is called a **tower**. A tower usually has around 15 giraffes. One is an adult male. The rest are adult females and young giraffes.

tower

Different towers usually get along with each other. They will sometimes even share the same land and food.

Glossary

calf

baby giraffe

ossicone

horn-like bump on a giraffe's head; covered with skin and hair

savanna

plains with scattered trees and a warm climate

tower

a group of giraffes; usually has around 15 members

Index

Credits

The images in this book are used with permission as follows. Images not listed here are © EDventure Learning LLC.

Cover and title page: Sian Cooper | Unsplash; Interior backgrounds: Kappy Kappy | Rawpixel; 3: Ronile | Pixabay; 4: Haily Sawyer | Unsplash; 5: Douw Jager | Dreamstime; 6: Simon Fletcher | Dreamstime (top), Dragoneye | Dreamstime (bottom left), macrovector | Freepik (bottom right); 7: David Mark | Pixabay; 8: Michael Bednarek | Dreamstime; 9: Wolfgang Hasselmann | Pixabay, zoosnow | Pixabay (inset); 10: Madison Friel | Unsplash; 11: Louise Pilgaard | Unsplash (inset), master1305 | Freepik; 12: Stingreal | Pixabay; 13: Siggy Nowak | Pixabay; 14: Laura Woodbury | Pexels, Designua | Dreamstime (map); 15: Designua | Dreamstime (map), Paula Joyce | Dreamstime; 16: Patrick Duvanel | Unsplash; 17: Olga Itina | Dreamstime; 18: Erich Röthlisberger | Pixabay; 19: Harshil Gudka | Unsplash; 20: Alexa Fotos | Pixabay; 21: Howard Wilks | Pixabay, Slawek K. | Unsplash (inset); 22: 5661282 | Pixabay; 23: Brian McMahon | Unsplash; 24: Yoni Kozminsi | Unsplash; 25: Peter Van Dam | Dreamstime; 26: Angie Gottling | Pixabay, David White | Unsplash (inset); 27: Mrs. Loretta R. Smith | Pixabay; 28 (from top): Dragoneye | Dreamstime, Stingreal | Pixabay, David Mark | Pixabay, Mrs. Loretta R. Smith | Pixabay

Printed in Great Britain
by Amazon

59071475R10017